Sultry Sea Slugs

COLORING BOOK

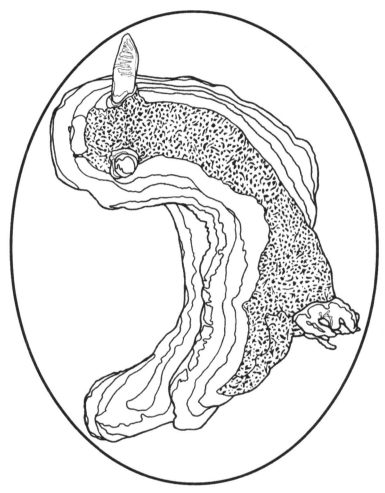

TWENTY THREE SEA SLUGS TO COLOR ANY WAY YOU LIKE

WWW.ALISONDNEVILLE.COM

ILLUSTRATED BY
ALISON NEVILLE©2019

Alison Neville 21

DIVE DEEPER INTO OR DISCOVER A LOVE FOR OUR OCEAN'S ECCENTRIC SEA SLUGS THROUGH TWENTY THREE
COLORING PAGES IN VARIOUS LEVELS OF DETAIL. A BLANK PAGE HAS BEEN ADDED BETWEEN EACH
ILLUSTRATION TO PREVENT BLEED THROUGH WHEN USING MARKERS.

OTHER TITLES INCLUDE: FUNGI FANCY AND SACRED SLOTHS

 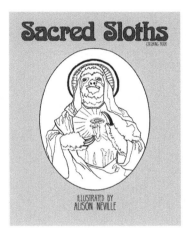

PUBLISHED 9/21/2019 BY

©ALISON NEVILLE

ISBN-13: 978-0-578-58293-1

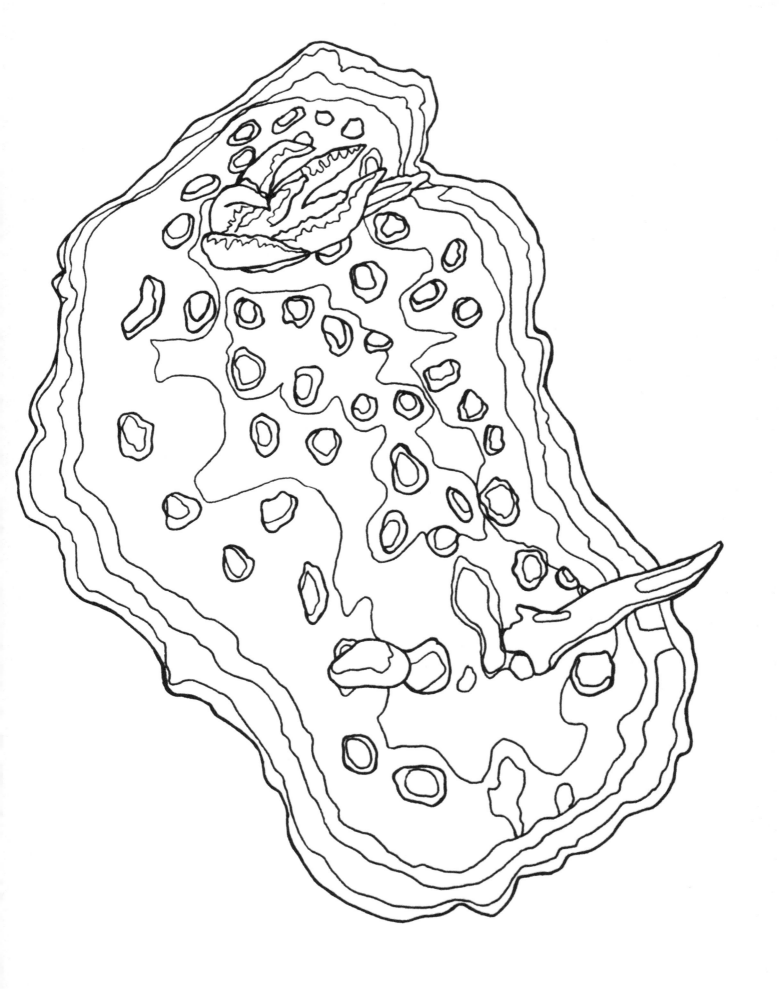

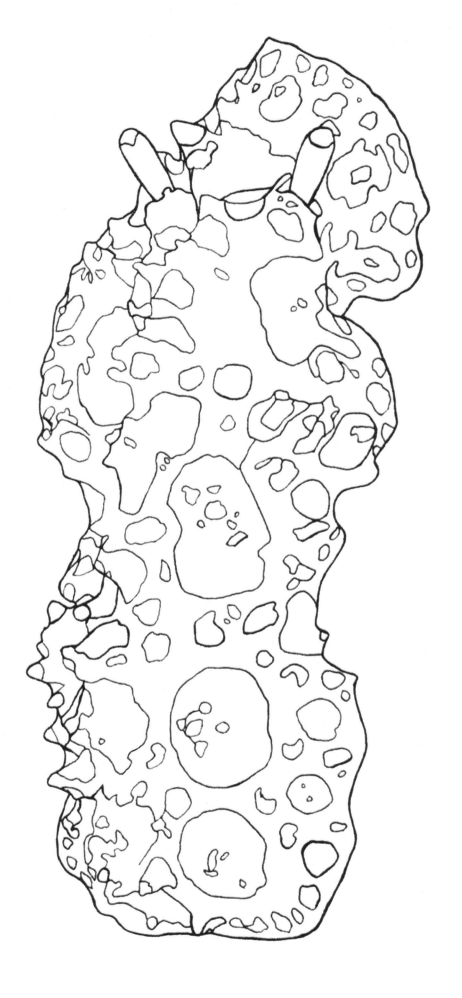

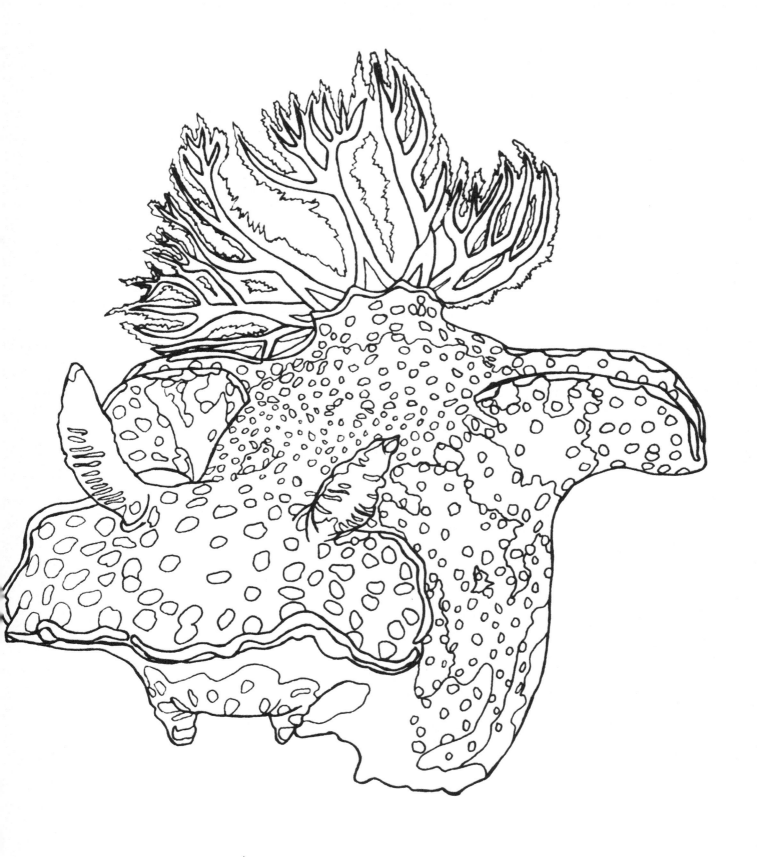

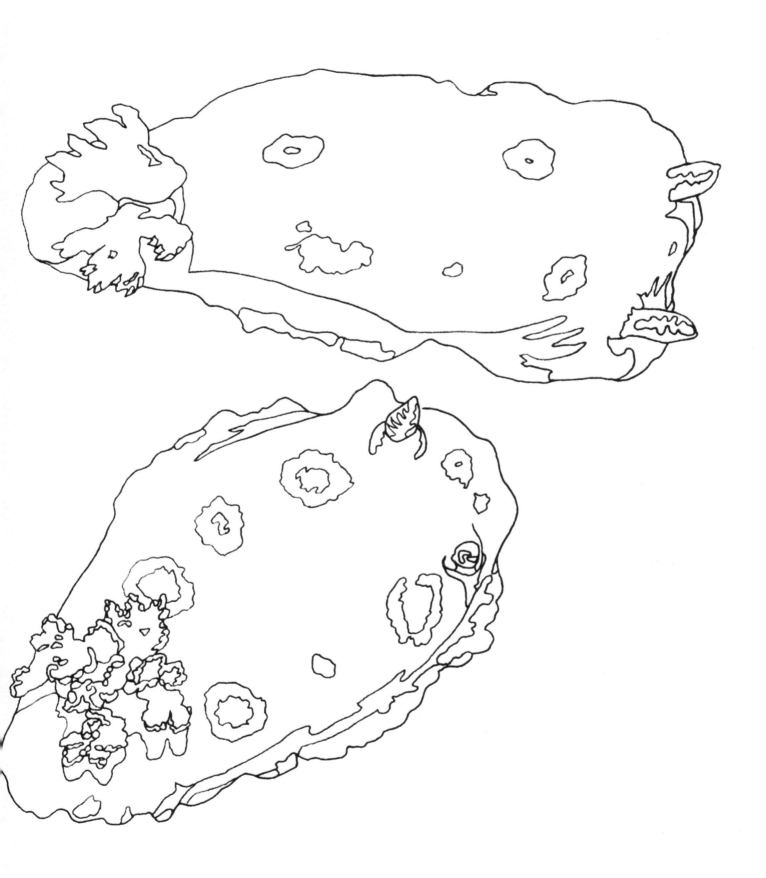

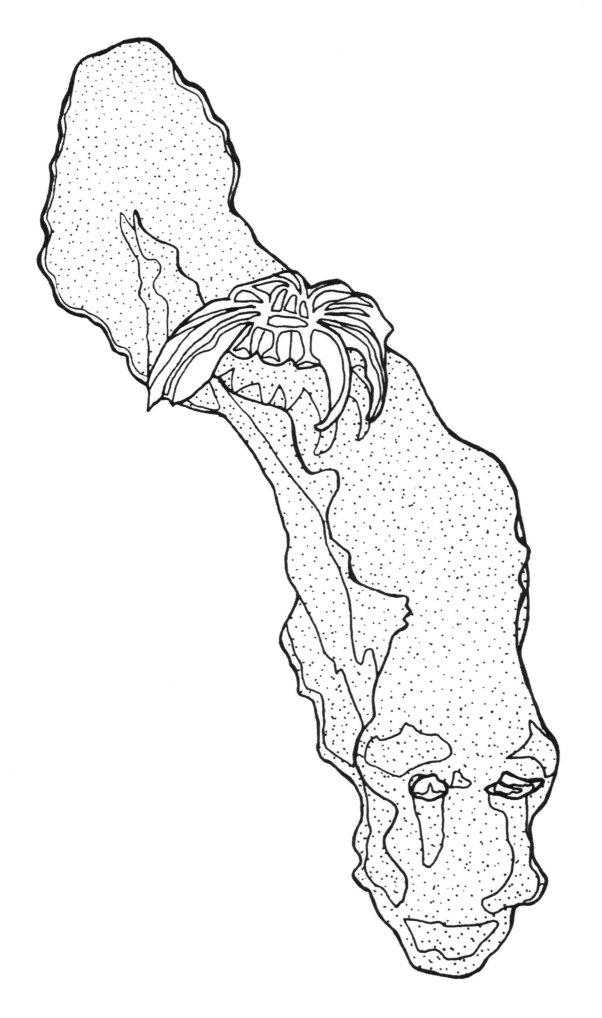

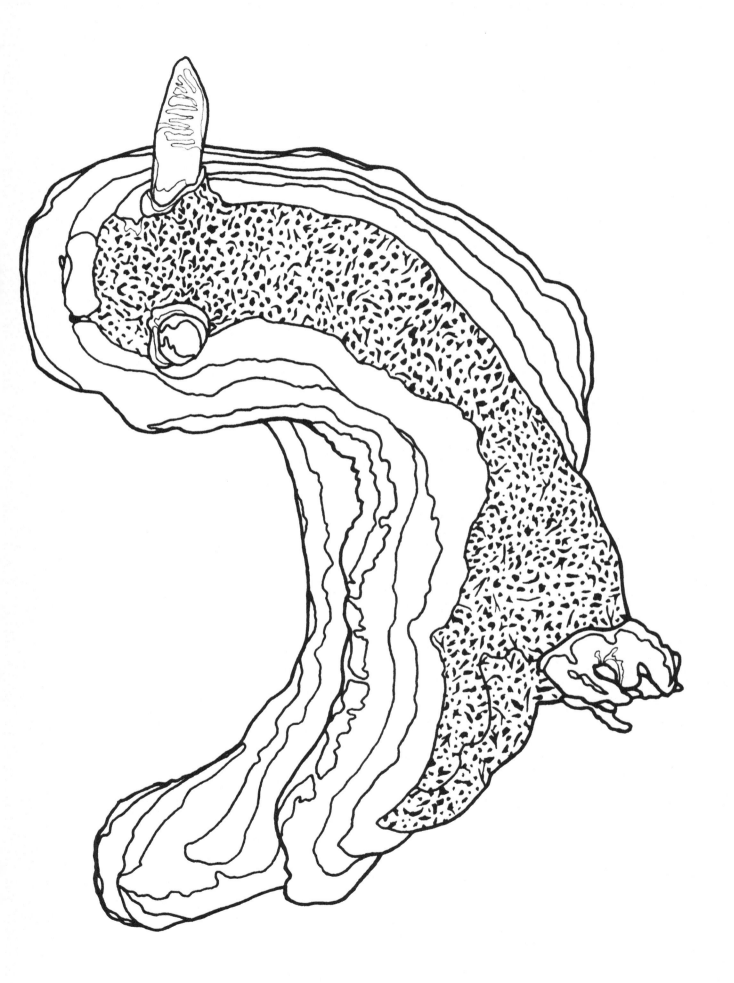

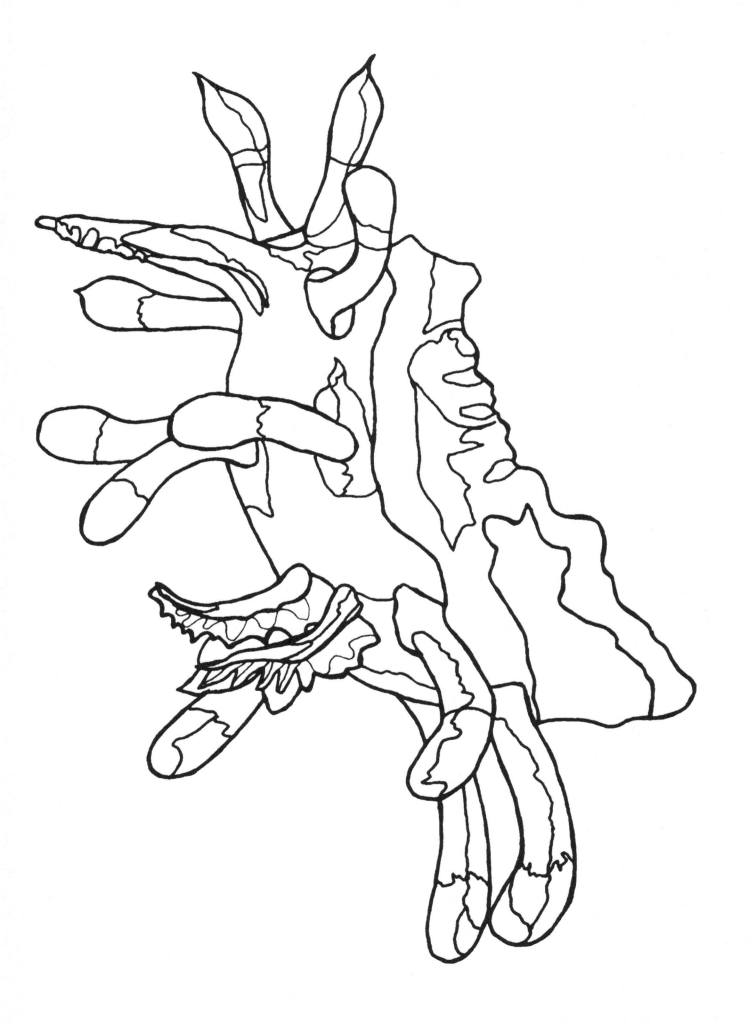

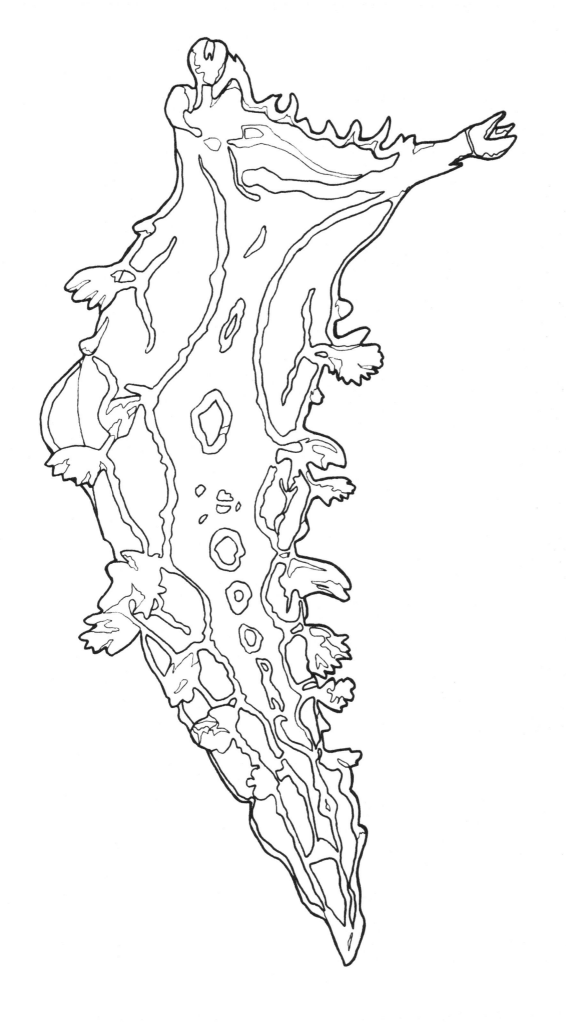

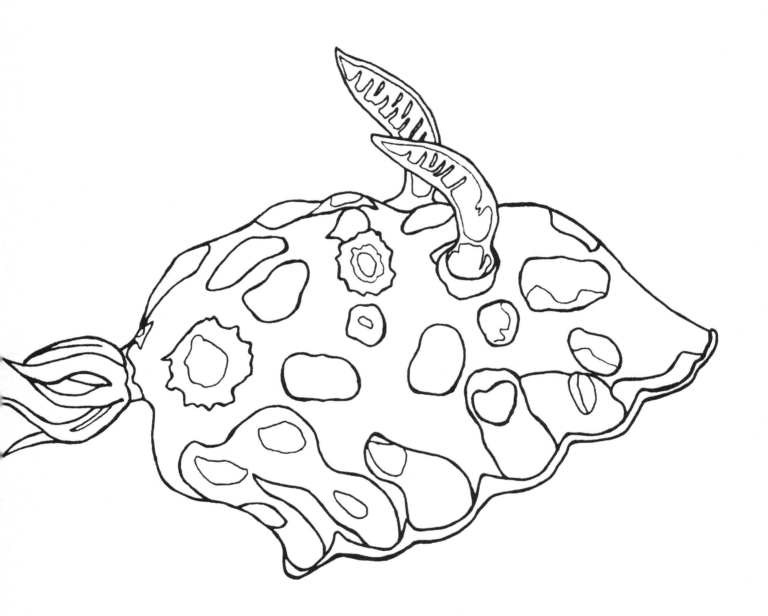

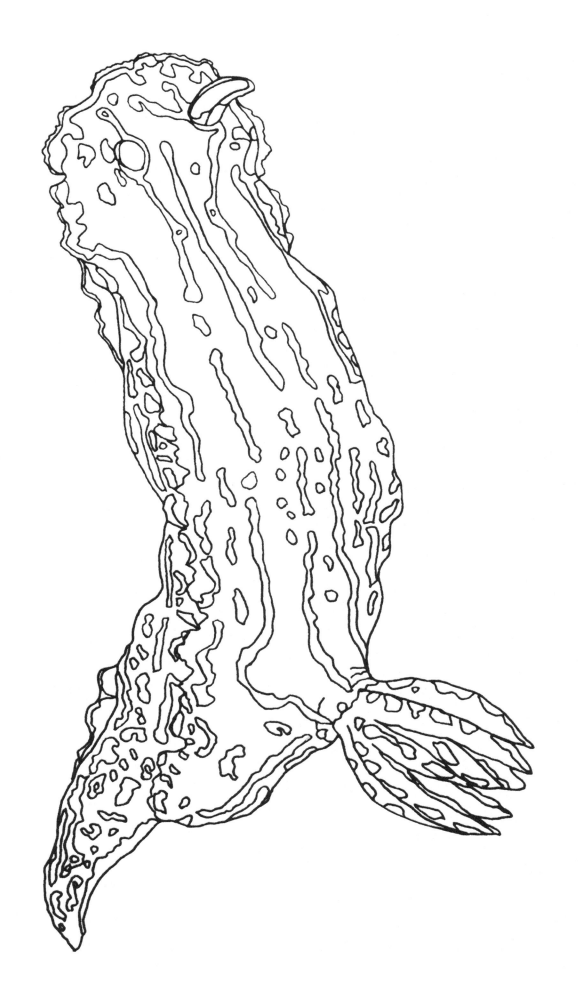

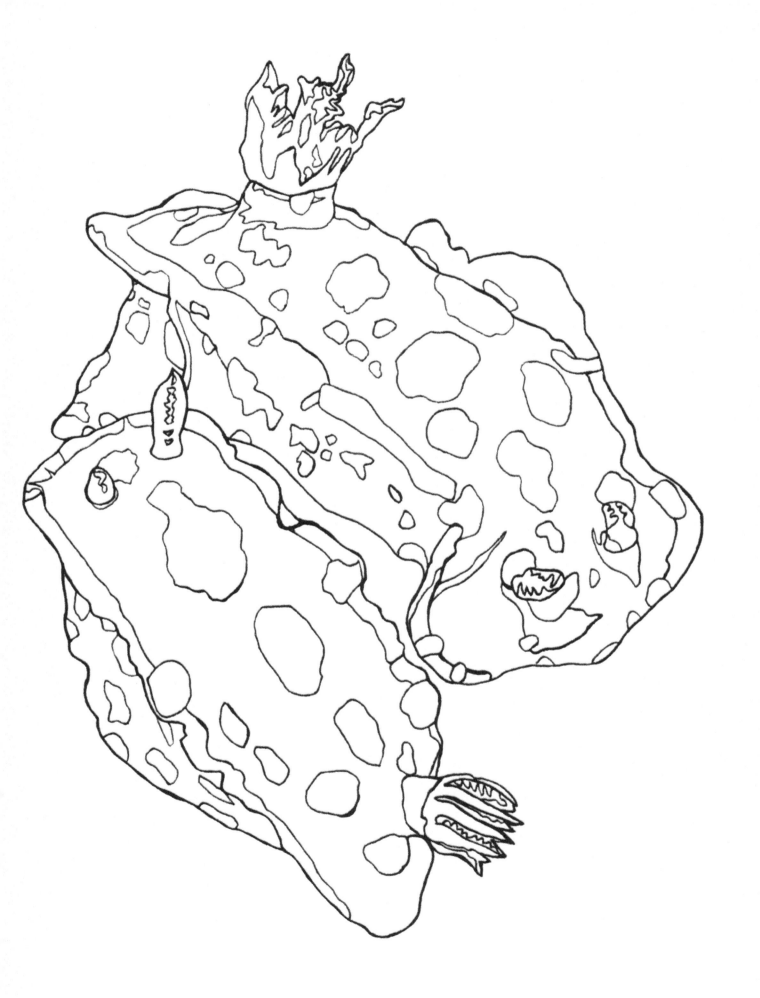

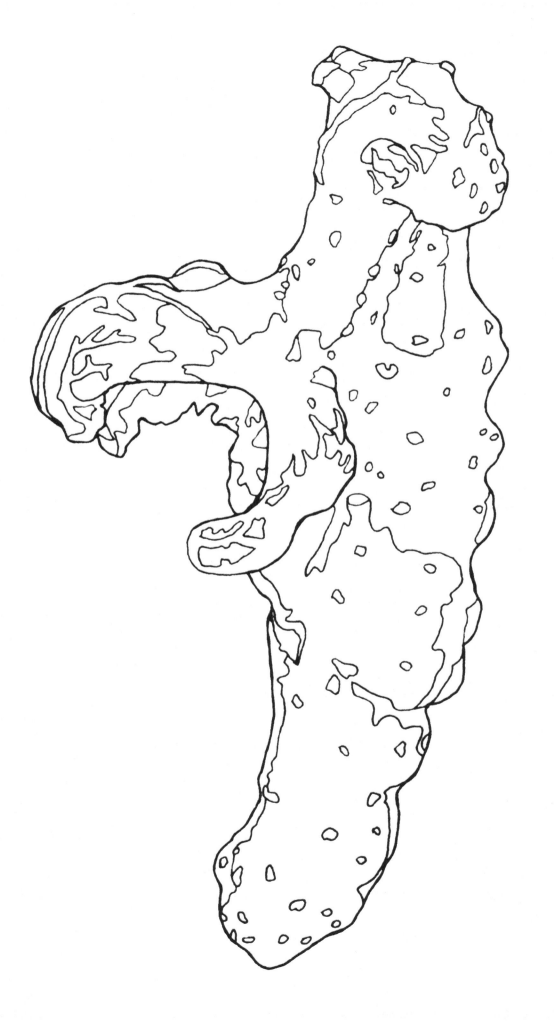

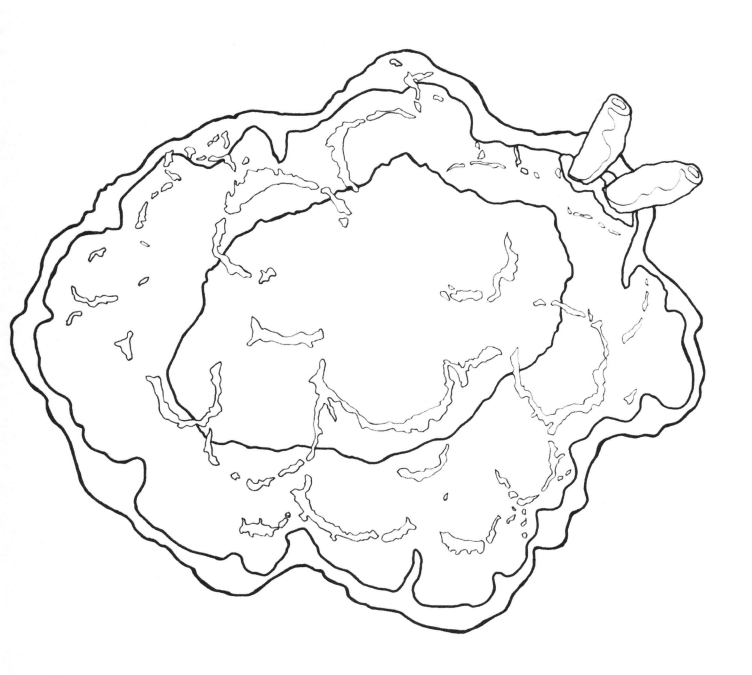

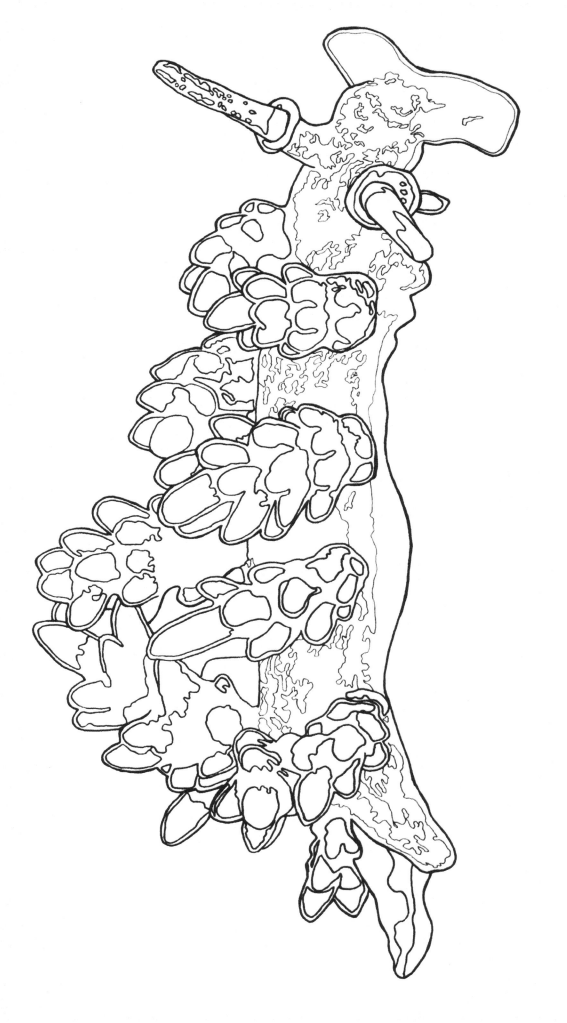

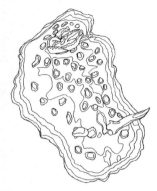

CHROMODORIS KUNIEI
DERIVATIVE OF "LEMBEH STRAIT..." BY
BERNARD DUPONT IS LICENSED
UNDER CC BY-SA 2.0

NEMBROTHA CHAMBERLAINI
DERIVATIVE OF "SEA SLUG
(NEMBROTHA..." BY BERNARD
DUPONT IS LICENSED UNDER CC
BY-SA 2.0

CERATOPHYLLIDIA
PAPILLIGERA
DERIVATIVE OF "PHOTO OF CER-
ATOPH..." BY NICK HOBGOOD IS LI-
CENSED UNDER CC BY-SA 3.0

GLAUCUS ATLANTICUS AND
GLAUCUS MARGINATUS
DERIVATIVE OF "BLUE SEA SLUGS..."
BY DOUG BECKERS IS LICENSED
UNDER CC BY-SA 2.0

ARDEADORIS EGRETTA
DERIVATIVE OF "FROGGIES LAIR"
BY BERNARD DUPONT IS LI-
CENSED UNDER CC BY-SA 2.0

CERATOSOMA TENUE
DERIVATIVE OF "CERATOSOMA
TENUE..." BY STEVE CHILDS IS
LICENSED UNDER CC BY 2.0

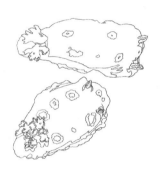

DIAULULA SANDIEGENSIS
DERIVATIVE OF "SAN DIEGO DORID..." BY
ED BIERMAN IS LICENSED UNDER CC
BY 2.0

GLOSSODORIS STELLATA
DERIVATIVE OF "MIKE'S POINT..."
BY BERNARD DUPONT IS LI-
CENSED UNDER CC BY 2.0

ELYSIA CRISPATA
DERIVATIVE OF "A LETTUCE SEA
SLUG" BY LASZLO ILYES IS LI-
CENSED UNDER CC BY 2.0

CHROMODORIS ANNAE
DERIVATIVE OF "SEA SLUG
(CHROMODORIS ANNAE)" BY
BERNARD DUPONT IS LICENSED
UNDER CC BY 2.0

OKENIA NAKAMOTOENSIS
REFERENCE IMAGE BY MONICA
VOLPIN

JORUNNA FUNEBRIS
REFERENCE IMAGE BY GUNTER
VANAPMEL

TRITONIA FESTIVA

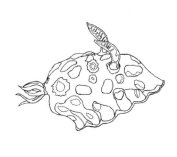

**CHROMODORIS
HINTUANENSIS**

**FLABELLINOPSIS
IODINEA**

TAMBJA MOROSA

**DORIOPSILLA
ALBOPUNCTATA**

FELIMARE PICTA

HALGERDA OKINAWA

CERATOSOMA AMOENUM

NOTODORIS SERENAE

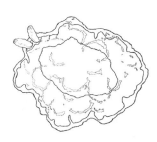

**PLEUROBRANCHUS
FORSKALII**

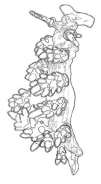

DOTO FLORIDICOLA

Made in the USA
Monee, IL
01 February 2021